D1536954

BIG WEATHER

Poems of Wellington

BIG WEATHER

Poems of Wellington

SELECTED BY

GREGORY O'BRIEN & LOUISE WHITE

MALLINSON RENDEL

Published in 2000
by Mallinson Rendel Publishers Ltd.,
P.O. Box 9409, Wellington

© Gregory O'Brien and Louise White, 2000
(selection and introduction)
The acknowledgements on pages v and vi
constitute an extension of this copyright notice.

Reprinted 2001, 2003

ISBN 0-908783-60-4

Photographs of Wellington by Anne Noble
Designed by Margaret Cochran
Typeset by Wordset Enterprises Limited
Printed by Bocarda Print Limited

ACKNOWLEDGEMENTS

Mallinson Rendel Publishers Ltd, Gregory O'Brien and Louise White
gratefully acknowledge the following authors, publishers and literary
agents for permission to include poems in this collection: Fleur Adcock
and Oxford University Press for 'The Greenhouse Effect'; Jackie Baxter
and Oxford University Press for James K. Baxter's 'Wellington' and
'The Maori Jesus'; Peter Bland for 'Wellington'; Jenny Bornholdt and
Victoria University Press for 'Bus Stop', 'Instructions for How to Get
Ahead of Yourself While the Light Still Shines' and 'We Will, We Do';
Bub Bridger and Mallinson Rendel Publishers Ltd for 'Wild Daisies';
James Brown and Victoria University Press for 'No Trick Pony' and
'Disempowering Structures in the New World'; Rachel Bush and
Victoria University Press for 'Stopping'; Kate Camp and Victoria
University Press for 'Unfamiliar Legends of the Stars'; Alistair Te Ariki
Campbell and Hazard Press for 'Houses at Night'; Geoff Cochrane and
Victoria University Press for 'Chaos on the roads'; Robert Creeley and
New Directions, New York, for 'Wellington, New Zealand'; the estate of
Eileen Duggan and Victoria University Press for 'Sunset', 'The Acolyte'
and 'Titahi Bay'; the estate of Lauris Edmond and Bridget Williams
Books for 'Round Oriental Bay', 'Summer Oriental Bay' and extract
from 'Wellington Letter'; David Eggleton and Auckland University
Press for 'I Imagine Wellington as a Delicatessen'; the Granville Glover
Family Trust for Denis Glover's 'Wellington at 5 o'clock', 'Wellington
Harbour is a Laundry', 'Wellington is a Shepherd's Pie' and 'Threnody';
Brian Gregory and Pear Tree Press, for 'Memory Harbour';
Dinah Hawken and Victoria University Press for 'Wellington', 'Today',
and extracts from 'Harbour Poems'; Sam Hunt for 'Walking the
Morning City' and 'Porirua Friday Night'; Cecelia Johnson for Louis
Johnson's 'City Sunday' and 'Song in the Hutt Valley'; Andrew Johnston
and Victoria University Press for 'New View' and 'Old Magnolias';
August Kleinzahler for 'Sunday Across the Tasman';
Fiona Kidman and Victoria University Press for extract from 'Speaking
With My Grandmothers'; Rachel McAlpine and Mallinson Rendel
Publishers for 'Energy Crisis'; Bill Manhire and Victoria University
Press for 'My Lost Youth' and 'Wellington'; Stephanie de Montalk and

Victoria University Press for 'Common Oak, Europe';
Michael Morrissey and Auckland University Press for 'Beautiful
Theories in the Capital'; Gregory O'Brien for 'Contents of a Breeze,
Wellington'; W.H.Oliver for 'The Streets of my City'; Bob Orr and Voice
Press for 'Wellington'; Chris Orsman and Victoria University Press for
'Ghost Ships'; Vincent O'Sullivan and Victoria University Press for 'July,
July'; Vivienne Plumb for 'Waitangi Day, Porirua'; Lindsay Rabbit for
'letter from holloway road'; John Ridland for 'A Ballad of IHC';
Bill Sewell and Pemmican Press for 'From Makara'; Iain Sharp for
'The Desperadoes'; J.C.Sturm and Steele Roberts for 'On the building
site for a new library'; C.K.Stead for 'The Immigrant Artist';
Robert Sullivan for 'Southerly'; Hone Tuwhare and Godwit Publishing
Ltd for 'Toroa, Albatross'; Ian Wedde and Victoria University Press for
'Here' and 'Podner'; Damien Wilkins and Victoria University Press
for 'Stage-Divers'; Louise Wrightston for 'Otari'.

Contents

'a window . . . full of houses'
Suburbs

'running away from its roots'
Parks, Bush and Beyond

The mists came drifting down the street,
With silken wings, with silent feet;
And suddenly on Lambton Quay,
There fell a veil of ecstasy.
The passers-by, the weary folk,
Put on the blue, enchanted cloak;
Their hurried ways grew grave and wise,
The dreams were naked in their eyes.
The golden wings of lamplight lay
Quivering on a world of grey,
And crooked streets climbed up the hill
To waiting gardens, wet and still.

Robin Hyde, 'Mists in the City'

In Cuba Street
When I was young
I bowled my hoop
Or whipped my top
And Time just loitered by.

Pat Lawlor, 'In Cuba Street'

It'll be fantastic when it's finished.

Billy Connolly
(when asked what he thought of Wellington)

Introduction

The gloriously various architecture of Tapu Te Ranga
marae at Wellington's Island Bay offers something of a
model for this collection of poems. Kaumatua Bruce
Stewart's inspired marae project has, he says, been con-
structed over the past twenty-five years from 'bits and
pieces of Wellington' – including doors from the old
Public Library, windows of all shapes and sizes,
Mitsubishi packing cases, boards, beams and other relics
of, to use Bill Manhire's phrase, 'the wooden town /
they've nearly finished tearing down / to make the city'.

Like Tapu Te Ranga, this anthology is a multifarious,
composite portrait, comprising 'bits and pieces of
Wellington' salvaged or borrowed from books and
periodicals. These poems chart a variety of responses to
the city, from euphoria to ambivalence to disdain. David
McKee Wright describes Wellington as 'the strong queen
city of the south'; James K. Baxter calls it the 'sterile
whore of a thousand bureaucrats'. Perhaps David
Eggleton is closest to the mark when he imagines
Wellington as a delicatessen, offering a kaleidoscopic
range of experiences.

Why does so much poetry emanate from
Wellington? Is it because of the city's bustling multi-
cultural existence, caught, as it is, mid-way between
Pacific Island and South Pole, between Small Town
New Zealand and South Seas San Francisco? Is it the
dramatic landscape? Or do the Dadaist configurations of
government, bureaucracy and life in general, offer the

1

necessary chaos out of which the poets can construct their own imaginative order? In the end, perhaps, the city is a prime site for diversity – and that's what writers feed on.

Most of the accounts gathered here are by inhabitants of the city – with a few interjections and rapturous responses from outsiders, including visiting Australian Henry Lawson and Americans Robert Creeley and August Kleinzahler. While the poems span the twentieth century, our centre of gravity is near the present. As the city has changed, its poetic reflection has kept pace – the city has got younger, the writing about it freer and wider ranging.

So, by the 1990s, we find Damien Wilkins at an inner city rock music venue, James Brown out on the cutting edge of consumerism – the New World supermarket, Island Bay – and Kate Camp contemplating the wind turbine on Brooklyn hill. While city, harbourside and suburban settings dominate much of the poetry here, in the final section we move beyond the Botanical Gardens and the Green Belt to explore Lower Hutt, Porirua and as far north as Plimmerton. If this collection offers a few dreams of escape, a little weather-induced anxiety and some dark, existential vistas, we hope it also captures something of the warmth and vitality of Wellington. Here we encounter the familiar place-names, landmarks and people, and the city's 'big weather' – to borrow Kleinzahler's phrase – which can only serve to quicken the steps and perk up the senses of the city's inhabitants.

GREGORY O'BRIEN & LOUISE WHITE

2

'canyon streets and trams'

Central City

Wellington

This is the place for a steep compact city.
This is the place to give you strength and palpitations,
the place to try and get and keep your balance in
    before you die.

The city buildings are primarily white and lie
    along a valley
from the enclosed harbour back to the rocky coast
which the arm leading into the enclosed harbour comes
from and belongs to, because a hand belongs
    to a heart.

The houses of the city are loosely built of timber
and corrugated iron to move with earthquakes
and each has been placed on, against
or below the inner ridge of hills surrounding
the enclosed harbour, which we hope will never go.

DINAH   HAWKEN

Walking the Morning City

Walking the morning city
the opposite direction
workers walking toward me
walking from the sun:
I have no job to go to
so walk into the station

watch the all-night Limited
pull in at the platform
pretend I'm waiting for
a friend who never came:
pretend I'm disappointed
vamp my blues harmonica

buy a lightweight pad
& biro at the station store
coffee at the cafeteria
pretend to write a letter:
have no one to write to
so drink a cup & leave

walk down morning streets
lightweight in the sun
no one to tell this to
'cause no one is my lover.
This morning more than ever
I'm set on finding you.

S A M   H U N T

I Imagine Wellington as a Delicatessen

I imagine Wellington as a delicatessen visited by
    Walt Whitman
and Allen Ginsberg, arm in arm like South Pacific
    sailors.
I imagine Wellington as a delicatessen, and Cook Strait
    as dancing
a Viennese waltz out of Walt Disney's *Fantasia*.
I imagine Wellington as a delicatessen enjoyed by
    the grey eminence
of Holyoake in the year of decimalisation,
    when Shindig dancers
did the Mashed Potato.
The delicatessen's airs are the pointilliste colours of
chopped, glazed fruit in cassatta desserts.
The delicatessen's airs are rainbows of steam
above shimmering haystacks of angelhair pasta,
and the lone, stern colossus choosing lunch at the
Captain Cook Exotic Salads Bar
is an heroic explorer discovering bell pepper
    archipelagoes,
or a small continent made out of pineapples.
I imagine foodies held gorgonised by Wellington as
    a delicatessen,
for not only do the pastry coffins of meat pies
no longer crack and flake,
maimed to dryness behind warming oven glass,
but the lollipop stoplights stay a sweet, sticky red,
while milkbar kids in white stetsons

twirl black lariats and ride out to Kilbirnie
on golden palominos of crumbling hokey-pokey.
If Karori's household spiderwebs are spin-doctored
        sugar,
and Parliament is a prosy palette of pastel creams;
then the Reserve Bank is all trim noughts of nougat,
and Courtenay Place is a squeaky, icing-sugared,
        Turkish delight.
The Xmas sponge trifle in every Pyrex dish rises
        to perfection;
the aroma of coffee, expressed just so, swirls up
to hills crowned by mock-cream clouds.
Lakes of milk, and orange juice waterfalls, give way
to charred barons of beef,
to charnel catafalques of mutton,
to fanfaronades of boutique beer.
I see scumbled peaks of Blue Vein cheese rising
over forests of perfumed licorice, scented vanilla,
        aromatic bergamot,
over creeks flowing with the bitter-juiced resins of
        cactus aloe,
over off-shore islands of tart lychee or globular loquat.
Sunlight white as vanilla ice-cream
slides along the clean curved tongue of the coast,
for the delicatessen is a temple of hygiene
lapped by aching green acres of billowing ocean.
I see Te Rauparaha with a bellowing conch, taniwha
        as Triton,
Olympic warrior on a pearlescent half-shell,
beneath rubescent skies which foam with stars,
like the stellar vintage of a Marlborough winery.

I see Bishop Colenso ascending to Heaven
above the catburglar clack of corrugated iron ridges –
free of the tangle of roots, trunks and blind staring
        shrubs
in every profane shadowy garden,
clear of the sodium auras of the assassinated night.
Tomorrow's Cinemascope dawn will flutter blue,
like slick cellophane Sellotaped by the fingers
        of the poet
across the gravy stains of fading things.
Tomorrow, the cracked King Edward fonts of
        the Miramar Palace
shall brim with rainwater in the silence of
        Armistice Day.
Tomorrow, new Odeons and old pagodas on
        Oriental Parade
shall be supported by reliefs of African pachyderms,
as a poppy blaze wreathes the charabancs of
        Manners Street
and Sunderland flying boats, carved from ice, wing it
        for evermore
over the baked Buicks and cooked Chevrolets of
        high summer.
The commissionaires of the soft drink concession,
the microwave wizards of the popcorn buckets,
will come into their own,
and the poppadam wafer, the pretzel stick,
        the halvah biscuit,
be held aloft.
A swimming pool split by an earthquake fissure
shall fill with boiling goat's blood,

as cupcake cupids cling to the copper cuspidors of
      Britannia Old Boys
and Cherry Coke cherubs chortle round
      Cuban humidors.
Tomorrow promises a fabulous Babylon
of suckling pigs and gelatinous ducklings
in the Wellington I imagine as a delicatessen.
In the Wellington I imagine as a delicatessen,
the capital is a cakescape on a glittering salver,
looped with festival garlands of bottlebrush tinsel.
Its piped icing is a woven tracery of gold threads,
whose vast pattern has an uncertain depth to it,
like reflections in a windowpane,
as translucent as yesteryear's parasols
caught in a sunshower on a Sunday promenade
      in Island Bay,
and turning the shallow yellow of lemon meringue pie.

DAVID EGGLETON

Wellington

Rugged she stands, no garlands of bright flowers
Bind her swart brows, no pleasant forest shades
Mantle with twining branches her high hills,
No leaping brooks fall singing to her sea.
Hers are no meadows green, nor ordered parks;
Not hers the gladness nor the light of song,
Nor cares she for my singing.
                              Rudely scarred
Her guardian hills encircle her pent streets,
Loud with the voices and the steps of trade;
And in her bay the ships of east and west
Meet and cast anchor.
                              Hers the pride of place
In shop and mart, no languid beauty she
Spreading her soft limbs among dreaming flowers,
But rough and strenuous, red with rudest health,
Tossing her blown hair from her eager eyes
That look afar, filled with the gleam of power,
She stands the strong queen city of the south.

DAVID   McKEE   WRIGHT

Wellington

A city of cenotaphs and tram-car sonnets ...
Broad-breasted town, thy swarded mounds
More numerous than Rome's ... We hang
Our houses out like washing to a breeze
That warns us of Scott's death-wish in the south.

The last colonial outpost ... Perhaps
The liveliest capital since the Vatican.
Arriving, anchored where Victoria's brigs
Banged bibles and brass cannon, I'd
Marvelled at hotels like pink casinos,

Wharves like sea-side cafés, terraced hills
Of rainbow-bright façades and cubist houses.
The gentleman's convenience in mid-town
I'd taken for a temple, and the people
Splashing in Oriental Bay seemed crowds

Of sun-gods spilt from a Picasso painting.
Let's blame it on the light! I stand
Committed to imaginary landfalls ...
The back door of a British council house
Could only lead out to the new Jerusalem:
Blake's burning bow was bound to scorch my hand.

PETER BLAND

The Immigrant Artist

Last night I met the Capital's captains of Art –
old Nugent Welch with his blue, watercolour eyes,
Colonel Carbery, Mrs Tripe. But Isobel Field
I'm told controls the purse-strings. She was heard to say
she thought me handsome – a pity my work was not.

This morning I climbed the streets. Paint peeled from
        boards,
iron rusted, concrete stairways cracked and slipped
and weeds pushed through. Part of me longed for
        home.
But scent of fennel and this hard unbroken light
on broken branches – they made me see fresh pictures.

From the Cable Car I looked down on a tumbling town,
a deep harbour, mysterious glittering hills.
The Colonel, the Tripe and the Field – all were dissolved
in air and light. No it's not the Promised Land
but a land of promise. I am choked with foolish hope.

C K S T E A D

1 3

On the building site for a new library

for Win

The machines moved in
On Saturday
Scraping the back lawn off
Like green paint
And the rose beds dead flat
Like they had never been at all
And shoved the blossom trees
Out of the way
So easily, you wouldn't believe –

    They had just started blooming
    Silly things
    Not knowing any better.

Come Monday
Linda stormed the cloakroom
Like a trooper
Swearing destruction of all bulldozers
And bureaucrats –

    The bastards
    The bloody obscene bastards
    Make me want to puke –

She told us
As we moved toward nine o'clock
Adjusting faces in the mirror
To look like nothing
Had happened
Shoving things into lockers
And images behind our eyes
Out of the way
Of duty –

      Roses unfolding in the morning sun
      People being peaceful under midday trees
      Grass growing emerald
      In the early evening light –

Thankful that we never knew
Didn't have to forget
Trees gardens buildings
Yes, even buildings
Before these ones
Or what the site was like –

      And could be again
      So they warn us –

When it was sea, all sea
And only sea.

J . C .   S T U R M

My Lost Youth

'My lost youth
as in a dream,'
begins this poem

beginning with a line
in what I think is Polish

*

glimpsed

on a sheet of paper
in the ticket-office
at the bottom of the cable car.

Two men behind glass
are bending over it,
the careful, mysterious

copperplate of Polish,
the English lightly
pencilled in above ...

Of course there is more to it
than my lost youth,

*

patches of pain and love,
a page from start to finish,

but you can hardly go on looking,
and tourists are lining up

*

and someone punches
your new downtowner

and through you go
and leave the poem behind –

keeping in mind a phrase or two
as you travel backwards up the hill

*

to alight at last

above the wooden town
they've nearly finished tearing down
to make the city ...

*

something about desire perhaps,
something about desire,
the fears ... or fires ... of youth,

*

'her mortal gown of beauty' ...

BILL   MANHIRE

Sunday, *Across the* Tasman

Big weather is moving over the headlands.
Turrets and steeples jab up at it
and the bank towers stand rooted,
logos ablaze at the edge of the earth.

In a suburban church basement the AA faithful
are singing hymns of renewal, devotion
and praise. He struggles with his umbrella
in the lobby of the Art Deco theater,

a dead ringer for the old 72nd Street Loew's
with its plaster Buddhas and kitsch arabesques –
the Preservation Society's last, best stand.
Young couples walk past hand in hand

as golden oldies flood onto the sidewalk
from the sweatshirt emporium next door.
His heart bobs, a small craft
awash for a moment with nostalgia.

Bartók liked to pick out a folk melody
and set it, a jewel in the thick
of hammered discords and shifting registers:
not unlike this dippy Mamas and Papas tune

floating along nicely among the debris.
The rain turns heavy, and the first
of the night's wild southerlies keens through,
laying waste the camellia and toi toi.

He wonders how the islanders managed
in their outriggers: if they flipped
or rode it through, plunging
from trough to trough with their ballast

of hoki, maomao, cod. Time for a drink.
A feral little businessman shakes
the bartender's left breast in greeting,
amiably, old friends.
                              Hi, Jack — she says.

Country people, he thinks, mistakenly.
The routines of home seem a lifetime away
and the scenes of his life rather quaint:
an old genre flick, never quite distinct

enough or strange to be revived
except on TV, and then only very late,

with discount-mattress and hair-transplant ads.

AUGUST KLEINZAHLER

Stage-Divers

Hell for leather is an odd phrase he
remembers only when standing at
the back of a rock concert with his
wife; their first gig in the three years
they've been married. A warehouse, an
improvised bar. Black and smoke.

She, too, used to like loud music and once
got around in a group of girls who fell
asleep inside the cabinets of concert
PAs. Fishnets and bright print dresses.

He was sometimes beaten up for his
jacket. His shoes, platform brogues with
fancy tongues, were also targets. Bought
from a golf pro shop out of town.

Things change, that's the song.
There is a child at home. He is the only thing
others now want of them and only then
sometimes.

As another kid launches himself,
his prone body passed from bruise to bruise above
their heads, they think one day when he is old
enough to carry a tune, they will hand all of
this up to him.

DAMIEN WILKINS

Wellington at 5 o'clock

Where they might stand and throw
Applecores down ship's funnels,
People walk dully home
Up steps, or go through tunnels.

DENIS GLOVER

Wellington

Time is a frown on the stone brow
Of a monument, a gale shaking the quay.
There is never time to let the whole day sink
Into the heart, and hold it sheltered there.

Power breeds on power in labyrinthine hives
Nested under the daylong driving cloud;
Stale breath of suburb dawn hazing the harbour,
Tiring the eye, stripping the nerve to fever.

City of flower-pots, canyon streets and trams,
O sterile whore of a thousand bureaucrats!
There is a chasm of sadness behind
Your formal giggle, when the moon opens

Cold doors in space. Here on the dark hill
Above your broken lights – no crucifix
Entreats, but the gun emplacements overgrown
And the radio masts' huge harp of the wind's grief.

J A M E S   K .   B A X T E R

The Streets of my City

The awning's slender pillars pace
Along the curving street.
Over a staggered row of shops
Outbuildings climb to meet
Sudden gorse-clad slopes.

A terraced road above the gorse
Climbs to a crest and falls
Down to iron rust roof slums
From green, sullen hills
Littered with wooden homes.

The empty-eyed turn in the wind
Like rubbish in a pool
From pub and job and boarding house
Through vacant streets until
It falters, and they cease.

W . H . O L I V E R

Stopping

I walked into my office one day and
Stopped.
Ah was the heart speaking,
Ah saying, morning has bust
the day in two and
the wind in the night has brought
down the bowl of honeyed water for the tui and
crashed it against the big clay
vase so its lip is broken.
The garden is assaulted by wind that brings
leaves and paper towels and receipts from
automatic tellers together and
drives two women, unwilling at the corner of
Molesworth and Pipitea Street, who lurch rush
into Keith Holyoake, his bronze statue arms.
It is a hurl-arch-sky, rush-whip-you and
dust-hurt-you day – and entering
the office you are afraid and stop.

RACHEL   BUSH

An M.P.'s Life for Me

Hi diddle dee dee!
An M.P.'s life for me!
You get the run of Bellamy's,
And pleasant trips across the seas.
Hi diddle dee di,
You've got to learn to lie,
And if your wife or mother lacks
The wherewithal to back the hacks
You just increase the income tax –
An M.P.'s life for me!

Hi diddle dee dee!
An M.P.'s life for me!
You get a car that calls at four,
With petrol coupons by the score –
Hi diddle dee do,
You ought to join the show;
The bars are open after six
And if you're landed in a fix
You blame it on the Bolsheviks –
An M.P.'s life for me!

Hi diddle dee dee!
An M.P.'s life for me!
You catch the strikers on the hip
By bringing in a censorship –
Hi diddle dee daw,
You influence the Law.

And if the people don't obey
In gaol you lock them all away,
Except, of course, the B.M.A.–
An M.P.'s life for me!

R O N A L D   L .   M E E K

The Desperadoes

Hand in hand we skip
down Molesworth Street.
It's good to be alone
in a capital city.
It's good to steal flowers
from the parliamentary gardens
while the ministers are in session.
Ah, look at your face.
You're as beautiful as jazz,
as jasmine.
We chuck pebbles
at the night sky.
Cracks appear in the moon.

I A I N   S H A R P

Wellington

It's a large town
full of distant figures on the street
with occasional participation.
Someone buys some shares,
another gets a piece of the action.
Foreign languages are spoken.
A good secretary
is worth her weight in gold.
The man himself
is sitting on a little goldmine.
And down on Lambton Quay
the lads in cars go past, it's raining,
and the boys from Muldoon Real Estate
are breaking someone's arm.
They don't mean harm, really, it's
nobody's business, mainly free
instructive entertainment,
especially if you don't get close
but keep well back like
all the distant figures in the crowd.
So you watch what you can
but pretend to inspect with interest instead
the photographs of desirable private
properties, wondering how close they go
to government valuation. That one's nice.
The question is, do you put your hands
above your head or keep them

in your pockets. Do you want a place
without a garage, could you manage
all those steps. The answer is
the man would simply like you off the streets.
You haven't even got a window
and his is full of houses.

BILL   MANHIRE

Vignette

Through the Autumn afternoon - I sat before the fire in the Library - and read - almost a little wildly.
I wanted to drug myself with books - drown my thoughts in a great violet sea of Oblivion.
I read about Youth - how the Young and the Strong had gone forth into battle - with banners of golden and blue and crimson. Of the sunshine that turned their processions into a river of colour - and the songs that, mellow and sweet, rose in their round throats.

I read of the young Painters - hollow eyed and pale - who paced their studios like young tigers - and with stupendous colossal ideas. How they sat together at night, in sweet companionship, round a fire - their cigarette smoke mystical, ethereal. And in the glowing coals was shadowed the beautiful flame-like body of Art.

And deeply I pored over the books of Youthful Musicians. Splendid - and tragic - and prophetic their faces gleamed at me - always with that strange haunted look. They had taken Life to them, and sung a Scarlet Song that had no ending and no beginning. And I read of all their resolves - and of their feverish haste, and the Phantastic Desires that sang themselves to birth … This and much more I read in my books.

Then all in a fever myself I rushed out of the stifling house - out of the city streets and on to the gorse golden hills. A white road ran round the hills - there I walked. And below me, like a beautiful

Pre-Raphaelite picture, lay the sea and the violet mountains. The sky all a riot of rose and yellow, amethyst and purple.

At the foot of the hill - the city - but all curtained by a blue mist that hung over it in pale wreaths of Beauty. No sound at all - and yet - the Silence of that Prophetic Atmosphere - that is created by the Twilight only. I leaned against a low paling fence - in my brain thoughts were clashing with the sound of cymbals. I felt Myself - by the power of my Youth - alone - God of it all.

Love and Fellowship - work and Delicious Fascinating Pleasures - must exist for me - if I only search for them. Away out in the harbour lights shone from the ships, and now in the city too - golden beckoning flowers.

There came a sound of slowly moving horses. I saw coming towards me a heavy carriage - slowly, slowly, coming towards me. And I stood still - and waited. The horses were hot and strained, the driver, muffled up to the eyes ... it was very cold. As it passed me I saw, inside, an old man, his head fallen back among the cushions, the eyes closed, the mouth half open, and hands of Age crossed before him. He was muttering to himself - mumbling, muttering.

Slowly it passed, and I watched it wind round the hill out of sight. I turned again towards the sea and the mountains - the City and the golden lights - but Darkness had rushed across the sky.

KATHERINE MANSFIELD

'the end of the earth's long breath'

Harbour and Sea

Round Oriental Bay

This is my city, the hills and harbour water
I call home, the grey sky racing over headlands,
awkward narrow streets that stirred me long ago
– it's half a lifetime since I first came in
wonderment and savoured here prodigious
conversations, gravid with abstractions, in Mount
Street cemetery; read Eliot; acted plays that
occupied us night long – planning, having visions,
making love with all the light sweet leisure
of the young till startled by the dawn we walked
still softly laughing to our dingy old addresses,
returning later for the talking, always talking,
in the drowsy gorse on Varsity Hill.

What else? The shared penury, our monumentally
naive political convictions; our cleverness
(the 'vicious little circle' marvelling at its
brilliance for a fragile funny summer term);
our simplicity – 'If you won't marry me
I'll wait for you for ever' – ah, it was all
for ever ... and now what's left of it, that
passion so intense there was a kind of moral
splendour in it, those helpless loyalties?

The bell of Saint Gerard's booms gently in the dusk;
the city's strict oblongs of light are new,
but in these hills the past is soaked like blood

that soaks a battlefield; the restless water grinds
the pebbled beach, before the island's dark hump
opens the winking red eye of the buoy; above me
lights wake too in gabled houses – the battered,
windswept, hill-top houses that still stand
and face the constant beating of the weather.

LAURIS EDMOND

Ghost Ships

If you look out at first light
you'll see on the harbour
the ships of our history
called back to life
by the sun's rekindling;
at dawn they discharge
guilty cargoes: ballast
spills in a gravelly bay,
musket cases, bayonets
wrapped in oilcloth,
are stacked on the shore.

There's a figure on the deck
dressed in serge, a high-
winged collar censures
his vision; he's taking the air
and whatever else
he can lay his hands on.

CHRIS ORSMAN

Beautiful Theories in the Capital

philosophy & ice creams & the choppy sea & old men
smiling in yellow raincoats   construction workers
from Babel's tower proud of their differing languages

one being self pity & a pigeon-necked walk   I've
seen it all before   because in a lifetime's walking
you glimpse the cripples   & their sun shielding

gestures so off-shore waders get wet under Oriental
Bay's very Occidental fountain   & nature before artifice
seems to win arguments in winter   well   this is April

& a high-heeled girl is reading her Lawrence beside
the untidy sea   what her white wrists mean is
                              anybody's
guess   how about the Chinese woman pulling weeds

in a purple hat   or a child hopscotching his mantra
in chalk   it's got to add up   & those   dark stones
visible beneath the sea   so much existence eggtimed

by a nod   the French say I bore myself   there could
be difficulties here   but over there a man has found
something alive and well in his shoes it could be

serious having a toe out of place   did you know
angels are drawing the unemployment benefit   that
                                                their
long silver wings caused a beautiful crash   yet no one

has death prepared right down to the last detail   the
        coffin
may be crammed with wonderful surprises low rent &
                                                such
a marvellous view   ah when it strikes we've had good
                                                chances

to catch the lion I mean scrub the lino   oceans may
look bald without fountains   I'm buying an ice cream
renting out the sea   that should cure philosophy

M I C H A E L   M O R R I S S E Y

from Speaking with my Grandmothers

The *Oriental* put down at Petone from where you
    were taken
by whaleboat to Evans Bay that spot
where merry ducks paddle their own canoes and darken
the clear shallows with their shit
your father brought
some books
a Gaelic bible
one or two willow pattern jugs
a blue embossed milk jug
a mahogany table
he took
one hundred acres of country
and one town acre fifty
chains of seafront at Lyall Bay
for some sovereigns and blankets
and beads and hatchets
and there's the rub
your legacy a ring a vase or two
and a label you couldn't
have dreamed I'd wear
and I've found only of late like a child
discovering illegitimacy in a certificate
hidden in the bottom of a knickers drawer,
the contrivances of that rush for the great land
grab before the Treaty of Waitangi was signed;
    we can thank

Gibbon Wakefield for that, the sailing ship
rushing down to Cape Verde Islands past the Cape
of Good Hope and on and on
through the harbour mouth
arrival: 30 January 1840
what a gasp of relief in the salons of London
we beat the bastards with seven days up our sleeves
look, you'd laugh if it wasn't serious,
as they say, the city mapped
out in tidy
lines
across a terrain as yet unseen by its planners
up hill
and down dale
well, no, up mountainsides
and down passes,
this town of ours kind of flattened
across the creases
of an imaginary map
a touch of parchment surrealism here
no wonder the lights
are wavering
all over the place
tonight
not a straight town at all

FIONA   KIDMAN

Here

A combination of exercise & insomnia is best
for keeping you in trim (falling in love
helps, but don't be surprised
if her response to your high condition
is a mixture of weariness & self-pity.
Well what did you expect, the
Liebestod from *Tristan?*

Study this sadness, give it some time,
it's real & it's 'just happening'
don't put it down
to autumn blues, in certain places the underground
cells of narcissi are preparing their banners
a wintering gannet slaloms the gales
down Evan's Bay, something else
is certainly going to happen

and one day in winter
you'll hear someone whistling
as you put your dawn coffee on
checking out that baleful glint in the clouds
listening with half your attention
to a jock babbling on the pre-breakfast programme.

As you go to work in the grey light
the cold breeze off the bays will pour down your throat
chippies & steel-fixers blowing on their fingers

as they jump
from the purple & red Fletcher Construction van
at the muddy Greta Point building site

a stink of diesel & fish will hit you
where some boat is up on the skids
getting her rust chipped

further on
by the new Hataitai Beach bathing shed
you'll notice a pale-blue item of underwear
chucked up on the toilet roof

at the Evan's Bay yacht marina
the same flash hulls will be wintering in their cradles
among rotten rope-ends and splashes of orange marine
paint

everything that is the same
will have changed while you weren't looking
and if you listen
carefully, around about now
you will hear
                that it's you
that's still whistling

IAN WEDDE

41

New View

Sea like a lake today,
strait like a door, water

leaving of its own accord.
Here's a new view,

a hill of shale for a lover to look over,
a slope, a slight rise, a house over-

looking the harbour, its
points of departure, a port.

Here's a boatload of hope held up by customs,
a courtship caught before the boat could sail.

ANDREW JOHNSTON

from **The Beaches**

II

Island Bay, Orongorongo, Day's Bay, Miramar,
Evans Bay where the slips and the rust-red ships are;
You can't lie still, pretending those are dreams
Like us ... Or watch, I'll show you: wet and clean,
Coming past the sand-dune couples, strung out far,
Purple on brown, his shadow grows between:
Bleached logs stare up: he's bringing us ice-creams.

ROBIN HYDE

The Maori Jesus

I saw the Maori Jesus
Walking on Wellington Harbour.
He wore blue dungarees.
His beard and hair were long.
His breath smelt of mussels and paraoa.
When he smiled it looked like the dawn.
When he broke wind the little fishes trembled.
When he frowned the ground shook.
When he laughed everybody got drunk.

The Maori Jesus came on shore
And picked out his twelve disciples.
One cleaned toilets in the Railway Station;
His hands were scrubbed red to get the shit out of
        the pores.
One was a call-girl who turned it up for nothing.
One was a housewife who'd forgotten the Pill
And stuck her TV set in the rubbish can.
One was a little office clerk
Who'd tried to set fire to the Government Buildings.
Yes, and there were several others;
One was an old sad quean;
One was an alcoholic priest
Going slowly mad in a respectable parish.

The Maori Jesus said, 'Man,
From now on the sun will shine.'

He did no miracles;
He played the guitar sitting on the ground.

The first day he was arrested
For having no lawful means of support.
The second day he was beaten up by the cops
For telling a dee his house was not in order.
The third day he was charged with being a Maori
And given a month in Mount Crawford.
The fourth day he was sent to Porirua
For telling a screw the sun would stop rising.
The fifth day lasted seven years
While he worked in the asylum laundry
Never out of the steam.
The sixth day he told the head doctor,
'I am the Light in the Void;
I am who I am.'
The seventh day he was lobotomized;
The brain of God was cut in half.

On the eighth day the sun did not rise.
It didn't rise the day after.
God was neither alive nor dead.
The darkness of the Void,
Mountainous, mile-deep, civilized darkness
Sat on the earth from then till now.

JAMES K. BAXTER

from **The Beaches**

VII

Cool and certain, their oars will be lifted in dusk,
       light-feathered
As wings of terns, that dip into dream, coming back
       blue; but the motionless gull
With his bold head, hooked beak, black-slit humped
       harsh back
Freezing in icy air gleams crystal and beautiful.
No longer the dark corks, bobbing bay-wide, are seen:
Dogs bark, mothers hail back their children from
       ripple's danger:
People dipped in the dusk-vats smile back, each stranger
Than time; each has a face of crystal and blue.

In the jettisoned boat, the child who peered at her book
Cannot lift her glance from the running silk of the
       creek:
It is time to return to her mother, to call and look ...
The sea-pulse beats in her wrists: she will not speak.
But the boats, in salt tide and smarting sunrise
       weathered,
Swing by an island's shadow: silver trickles and wets
The widening branch of their wake, the swart
       Italian faces,
Fisherman's silver fingers, fumbling the nets:
And the island lies behind them, lifting its glassy cone

In one strange motionless gesture, light on stone:
Only the gulls, the guards of the water-lapping places,
Scream at the fishermen lifting the water-lifting nets.

Far and away, the shore people hear a singing:
Love-toned Italian voices fondle the night: the hue
Of the quietly waiting people is velvet blue.

ROBIN HYDE

Wellington Harbour is a Laundry

The harbour is an ironing board:
Flat-iron tugs dash smoothing toward
Any shirt of a ship, any pillowslip
Of a freighter they decree
Must be ironed flat as washing from the sea.

Though steamed up hot, small tugs do not
Refrain from treating a liner as a counterpane.
They flatten anything that floats, and try
To iron out ships until they're dry,
And while we stand and look, land-lubbered,
Fold them alongside in the linen cupboard.

The Harbourmaster, creased like a lord,
Laundry-manages for the Harbour Board.

DENIS GLOVER

Wellington Harbour — a Shepherd's Pie

Water assumes cooking colours as the sun
Directs the unwilling downcast clouds
To pattern it constantly in change.

Wishing to take orders from none,
They call the sun a hotted kitchen range.

So does the harbour, flat as the flat sky,
Both lightly scarified, a shepherd's pie,
The one transiently scored by a ship's wake
The other an inverted casserole deep-bake.

Beneath the sky the clouds are never idle:
The harbour remains indifferently tidal.

DENIS GLOVER

from **Harbour Poems**

The harbour is hallucinating. It is rising
above itself, halfway up the great
blue hills. Every leaf of the kohuhu
is shining. Cicadas, this must be the day
of all days, the one around which
all the others are bound to gather.

The blue agapanthus, the yellow fennel, the white
butterfly, the blue harbour, the golden grass,
the white verandah post, the blue hills, the yellow
leaves, the white clouds, the blue
book, the yellow envelope, the white paper.
Here is the green verb, releasing everything.

Imagine behind these lines dozens and dozens
of tiny seed-heads whispering. They are a field
of mauve flowers. What they say is inexplicable
to us because they speak another language, not this one
written from left to right across them, made up of
distinct and very subtle, ready-to-burgeon sounds.

The harbour is disappearing. It is giving up
all the decent distinction
between itself and the grey hills and sky.
But a line of light, a line of white hope has
        suddenly come
along the opposite shore, and now, since like everything
else it cannot last, it is leaving.

The karo has thrust one branch – which becomes
      four others,
the highest one with a green flower of leaves round
a white centre at the top – above the taupata.
It seems to be saying hooray, look at this,
wow, incredible, I've done it! It's not though,
is it? It's not saying anything.

How can you wait quietly on this calm day
with rain falling straight down pounding nothing
but the odd light leaf on a soft stem standing
in the stillness? The scene is in grave danger.
The birds know that. How on earth can you settle
      into yourself
– like a small pond – when there's wind in the wings?

DINAH HAWKEN

Wellington

The city
white with rain

a merging
alphabet of stone.

Soundlessly a seagull
flew past my window

the single arc
that hours

of wind
could not disperse.

The rain
sewed small oblivions

on the tide.

B O B   O R R

The Greenhouse Effect

As if the week had begun anew –
and certainly something has:
this fizzing light on the harbour, these
radiant bars and beams and planes
slashed through flaps and swags of sunny vapour.
Aerial water, submarine light:
Wellington's gone Wordsworthian again.
He'd have admired it –
admired but not approved, if he'd heard
about fossil fuels, and aerosols,
and what we've done to the ozone layer,
or read in last night's *Evening Post*
that 'November ended the warmest spring
since meteorological records began'.
Not that it wasn't wet:
moisture's a part of it.

As for this morning (Friday),
men in shorts raking the beach
have constructed little cairns of evidence:
driftwood, paper, plastic cups.
A seagull's gutting a bin.
The rain was more recent than I thought:
I'm sitting on a wet bench.
Just for now, I can live with it.

FLEUR ADCOCK

from *Wellington Letter*

I

Five o'clock; the winter morning's
no more than a bleak frontier
of the night. This rough hill, where
houses tilt to the tides of the rowdy
dark, gives just a hand-hold; we're
tossed among squally showers 'moderate
swell to the west, wind 20 to 30 knots'
— the marine forecaster's voice brings
a map of rainy seas, Kapiti to Cape
Palliser, Cape Palliser to Puysegur
Point, visibility 4 knots (from Stephens
Island to Jackson Bay the seas are
slight). And Nugget Point? He burrs,
knobbed as a knotted rope, a chunk
of cliff chops into the misty vision
slapped by a moderate southerly swell.
We rock into the windy morning. Yesterday
Evans Bay was a city of slim white ships.
I thought of you. Voices. Voices.

LAURIS EDMOND

Podner

(for Bob)

There are no wekas in Weka Bay
nor is this a poem about
ecology. Bob
is sitting in the next room
looking at moonlight on Evans Bay
he's listening to the sea
& to the wind in the macrocarpa trees
& noting the lights of Mt Crawford Prison
& of the defence base at Shelly Bay.
In this room I am doing exactly the
same. It's a view that packs it in.
It's even better than drugs or alcohol
or the hectic pulse of your favourite fantasy
for getting you into the mood to write
exciting poetry. A combination of all four
is generally too much: stupefied
we make coffee & wonder whether youth
isn't an ephemeral
mental condition. But now
we have both suddenly begun pounding on our
typewriters. It sounds as though Bob
is pounding on his desk as well.
Now he puts on a record of Boris Godunov
& bites the bung from a flask. The moonlight
drops its bins of broken bottles on Karaka Bay.

In
Balaena Bay
the pinkish severed heads of strange fish
are rolled about by little wavelets.

IAN WEDDE

Today

It's a calm day on earth, almost silent.
Only the birds are singing.

Why don't people go down to the harbour,
stand at the end of the earth's long breath
and listen?

DINAH HAWKEN

'a window ... full of houses'

Suburbs

Bus Stop

I

At the bus stop we are fascinated by everything.
Trees on the hill above
the wind in them
everyone else coming from all directions,
          diving out from streets
around the hillside, emerging from cars,
       coming up the road, all
with the bus stop in mind.
We cluster around it waiting fresh from our beds
       waiting beside
others fresh from their beds everyone fresh and
       clean and ironed
and wind-blown gathering their clothes around them.
And we are interested in everything – the coat
       worn by the man
and the shoes worn by the woman and
       the falling down socks of the
young girl with the beautiful face.
And when the nice woman tells the young man
       he has left his
parking lights on we are overjoyed with the drama of it
       all, crane
our necks, follow him down the road with our eyes,
       want to clap a
little, say   what grace   what style.

2

Look out all around you
the trees grow before our very eyes
turn into forests we could get lost in.

Having done that, having lost
the bus stop and the others waiting at it
we would then be alone in the forest
wandering about
and would be grateful, joyful, at stumbling across
     a fellow passenger
we would discuss our most vital needs with
     these strangers
saying   *food   water*   in reverential tones
and we would ask the most
important things of each other
like – I have cut my hand, please, would you
     bind it for me.

JENNY   BORNHOLDT

July, July

There's a dreary morning coming up,
the sky's as dull as a shoe.
It'll be a day that won't touch
even the last gasp of blue.

The best words won't work –
love and the rest, love
and the glint it's meant to give,
love's as slack as an old glove.

The harbour lies there meek
in a window looking south,
the south and its imagined fangs
in that imagined mouth.

'That'll be the day' as we like
to say, but it won't be today,
'There's a dreary week of it coming up,'
is what we say, and say.

Yet a day when you don't expect it,
sheer glitter ringing about
as if all the cutlery drawers of Kelburn
had been tipped out,

a day when the knives don't nick,
when the dry horizons scale.

There's a shine and flicker to the wind,
southern rancours fail

to cut the ice we expect,
the mountains ride their horses
with their withers of snow,
and the wind, the stroked manes of the horses.

VINCENT O'SULLIVAN

Contents of a Breeze, Wellington

September 1990

Elaborate forms of urban life, Wellington: swirling trees
aeroplanes pass between, a freshly mown lawn
     arriving from
three blocks away. As Eastern Europe heads west,
     school parties
raise and lower the Green Belt, a tour bus vacates
     the mountainside
and our rubbish bin which disappeared southwards
     five days ago
returns, clattering, rolling in from the north-east.

GREGORY O'BRIEN

No Trick Pony

The plain words – the best ones –
you couldn't give them away.

On the edge of the suburbs, it becomes hard
to come up with

other options – the skies so blue
you can hear yourself think.

More and more, closeness is required,
the collusion of cheek against stone.

Instead, the serene lawn mower,
who might be the both of us, circling into sleep.

JAMES BROWN

letter from holloway road

the evenings are drawing out
movement is more pronounced

late sun makes an eye sparkle
a lip slips across foliage

currency is exchanged
at gateways

light wets tongues ...
even the silent are articulate

LINDSAY RABBIT

Disempower Structures in the New World

A 2-litre bottle of Diet Coke
from the local dairy costs $3.50,
whereas a 2-litre bottle of Diet Coke
from the New World supermarket
round the corner costs $1.95.

A short walk therefore
through the new maths
appraises the situation, viz:

$$
\begin{aligned}
& \$3.50 \\
&-\ \ \$1.95 \\
&=\ \ \$1.55
\end{aligned}
$$

where $1.55 approximates
net consumer loss, as well as
– on a different calculator –
potential retail profit.

You decide this knowledge is
'not cricket', but bottle it,
resolving – tomorrow – to visit
the New World supermarket
and then make the dairy owner an offer
of 2-litre bottles of Diet Coke
in a scenario rendered thus:

```
    $2.65  ergo      $3.50
 −  $1.95          −  $2.65
 =  $  .70¢        =  $  .85c
```

where 70c represents your portion
of the aforementioned
potential retail profit ($1.55)
− now redistributed
under new management.

If only you'd gone straight to the New World
− it also being open late every night,
thanks to the job-eager energies
of youth-rated young people, who will
still squeeze out smiles at 5 minutes to 10
and ask you if your day's going well.

Tonight, however, the dairy owner too
is (for once) unusually cheerful
as he accepts your money, chatting
about the cricket and asking
what it is you do.
'I'm in education,' you vaguely volunteer,
thinking of that final year for your BCA.
'Education − a good job, eh?' he says,
and asks about the pay.
'Mmm, 25 to 30 thousand,' is your dim reply.
'Yes, good job, good money,' he says,
'good money' shining in his eyes.

But now a child in pyjamas
is wailing, and he is talking
in another language, lifting her
onto the counter, while you are
hurrying home, checking
your change, counting
the silver stars in the night sky,
which are all lucky
and are all yours.

JAMES   BROWN

There is chaos on the roads

There is chaos on the roads.

It is winter in Khandallah;
It is winter in Kilbirnie.

Rain leaps in a spray
From streetlamp to streetlamp;
Wind gusts with a hoot through wires.

She doesn't want me, no,
But what do I do with her ghost,
That yellow hint of herself
She has failed to take with her?

There are wormholes in time.

There is darkness over an ocean.

GEOFF COCHRANE

Houses at Night

One by one the houses slip their moorings.
They drift aimlessly, nosed by cars
attentive as pilot-fish.
They loom up blank as barges.

It's light that makes a clearing in the night
on which the muscled darkness leans in vain.
It's light that ties the houses to the ground
and without light they soon would float away.

Past midnight and the houses have all gone.
Light from a passing comet fastens on my brain
and swings it round and round ...
It snaps – and I hurtle into sleep.

ALISTAIR TE ARIKI CAMPBELL

Instructions for How to Get Ahead of Yourself While the Light Still Shines

If you have a bike, get on it at night
and go to the top of the Brooklyn Hill.

When you reach the top
start smiling – this is Happy Valley Road.

Pedal at first, then let the road take you down
into the dark as black as underground
broken by circles of yellow lowered by the street lights.

As you come to each light
you will notice a figure
racing up behind.
Don't be scared
this is you creeping up on yourself.
As you pass under the light
you will sail past yourself into the night.

JENNY BORNHOLDT

Energy Crisis

Now I've settled down again.
Reward me: send me away.

Some days Wellington behaves –
the air is sedimentary
and workmen smoke on girders
and forget to demolish Lambton Quay.
One for the sauna,
one for the Scripture Union.

I know we're all God's children.
I reserve the right to say
I don't care how left wing you are,
if you're going to be a paranoid cynic
I'd rather have a motorbike
or a polyanthus, thank you.

But the wind is our prophylaxis here –
we need the wind to suck the shit away
or we'd never do a thing beyond
renovate, regurgitate,
lock the turbulence indoors
because we're all so terribly mature.

I'm always going on about clouds
but look, on Tinakori Hill
we've got very fast weather.

We do have sun, but it flirts
and nobody dwells on that,
and our hair is rightly pulled
by flying water.

The point is moving fast and often,
diving up the air, inventing blue,
all of which alters the prospect.
I am opposed to closeness, which
implies being met at the airport.

The world is improving:
look at apples and underwear.
My grandmother called me a peasant
with my potato hands. It's much
like being no lady, but a woman.

The children do their duty all the time.
The big ones make a noise, that's their job.
They talk by colliding and they don't break much.
The tiny children visit on their microdots
and write important letters to the Queen.
And the very large ones do assignments
and withhold significant truths
about boyfriends and girlfriends,
and their baths are very long but they all
have the right sized laugh.

None of them knows about benzene or bowsers.
They do not repeat themselves.

May the children grow up? No they may not.
They must do assignments forever.

And one says, 'Lo, I am fluorescent.'
I'm more keen on the rough ones,
not for themselves but because their job
is liberating rivers and they walk on eggs.
They wear their clothes like a boat.
They're the only buoyant saviours
in flip flops and punctures,
defending the ends of the earth,
pathologically heterodox and fizzy.

There's nothing to hide:
that's how I know it's spring.
Every hour the punga pops a G-spot,
rapidly getting unknotted.

Leave me alone. I can swim.
I harbour a lake of Bach,
the Tinakori jig revs up inside me –
nothing fancy, mind you,
just a tree of roaring feathers
in revolt.
Remember a woman's multiple stem:
it's all physique,
the phrases queue like breakers
and their shapely echoes.
Don't you see? It's no contest –
I'm overboard, I'm going,

I'll be back before tomorrow,
I'll give you the news of the world
when I get back.

RACHEL McALPINE

Sunset

Low over Tinakori
The west droops on the town.
What if on Tinakori
The blazing sky fell down!

Would all the folk float golden
Like rocking fleets of Tyre,
Or would they, felled by wonder,
Fall wound in cloth of fire?

EILEEN DUGGAN

We Will, We Do

Meet your grandfather Henry Eugen (Harry)
as a young boy on the Oriental Terrace
zigzag. He's on his way home to
McIntyre Avenue after swimming in
the salt water Te Aro baths, laughing
and laughing, running home to tell
his brothers about the octopus getting in
to the pool through the pipe.

Running down Majoribanks Street on a day in 1912
on his way to work as a lolly boy at the Opera
House.

On his way to grow up and leave school at 13
start his mechanical and general engineering
apprenticeship. Eager. Runs towards
the bridges he will build. Spends five years as
an apprentice and one as a journeyman
emerges at the start of the Orongorongo
Tunnel in 1922 and begins work.

Again you see him
on his way to design the Thorndon pool
where your sister now swims in her bluegreen cap
a wave moving through the water.

Here he is studying the one
white shoe abandoned on the zigzag.
It's been there for weeks, the colour slowly
leaking into the concrete. A woman's shoe.
Next time you see him he's on his way to marry
your grandmother who has only one leg and on it
one white shoe.

JENNY BORNHOLDT

Summer Oriental Bay

The salt dark is full of voices
words that rustle along the boulevard
or float
furred like moths
about these tall lamps

the small restaurant
yellow-lit and nautical in style
bears its painted ropes and anchors
over a rocking tide

wind in the norfolk pines sings
its formal melodies above
our brief encapsulated happiness

but the stars laugh
running high and fast above a black horizon.

LAURIS   EDMOND

'running away from its roots'

Parks, Bush and Beyond

City Sunday

The jaunty straws, the Sunday hats
Stroll blandly from the Government flats,
Their plastic fruit and flowers of glass
On heads as dark as beaten brass
Gleam in the sun: sedate beside
Blue suits, white collars, quietly stride.

Ahead of them, like nylon fawns,
Two skirted children eye the lawns
For weekday running: now green grass
Wears an ironshod word — 'Trespass.'
But like cicadas in the trees
The band ahead has news to please.

Its solemn notes rise thin and clear
Upon the neutral Sunday air
Where even buses learn to mute
The rancour of their usual route
And rising bush absorbs all sound
Before it gets above the ground.

One pair of high heels on the path
Creates the only hint of wrath
To crack the windows of this view
As goes a girl, all limbs, and new
To old designs and repetitions
That may restore the lost positions.

But she has vanished through the trees
And eyes revert through stone degrees
As the band turns the page to surge
Onwards through its ponderous dirge,
And suits and hats arise, resume
Their walk, then home to habit's room.

LOUIS   JOHNSON

Common Oak, Europe

Botanical Gardens

The trunk of *Quercus Robur*
is running away from its roots.

It has crept across the lawn
to the fence
where it has raised itself
on a bleak elbow

in search of an identity
more in keeping
with its neighbours.

Its dependable heart
is no longer in ship building –

hydrokinetics, hydrostatics
and the science of structure
have affected the value
of its hulls –

and demand for strength
and crafted excellence
in furniture
is fading –

no one makes hollowed seats
and massive bookcases
any more

tea tables in Chinese taste
ribbon-backed chairs of Rococo design

and the fretwork and pagoda cabinets
with glazed shelves
so successfully adapted
by Chippendale
for the display of wine and water
containers
and included in his cabinet-making directory

are only seen in museums now

brass nails
turned posts
and spindles are out

frames fringed with leather
and decorated with velvet
are rare

and there has been a decline
in the ancilliary arts
of marquetry
and gilding

even Country Furniture
once thought to be
plain and provincial
has become an endangered species.

*

So it waits –
patient
hardy
uniformly dignified
despite its obvious age –

wondering why the move
to haste
and replication

wondering whether life would be better
as a willow oak
tulip oak
or river oak

accepting that an airy
and ornamental image
is not necessarily a substitute
for the setting of oars
and the gathering of winds
in ancient seas

knowing
that mention of European ancestry
although helpful
is unlikely to carry weight
in a garden of tree ferns.

STEPHANIE DE MONTALK

Wellington, New Zealand

'That's the way
(that's the way

I like it
(I like it'

·

Clouds coming close.

·

Never forget
clouds dawn's
pink red acid
gash–!

·

Here comes
one now!

·

Step out into
space. Good
morning.

·

Well, sleep,
man.

·

Not man,
mum's
the word.

•

What do you
think those hills
are going to do now?

•

They got
all the
lights on –
all the people.

•

You know
if you never
you won't

2/29/76

It's the scale
that's attractive,
and the water
that's around it.

•

Did the young
couple come
only home
from London?

Where's the world
one wants.

•

Singular,
singular,

one
by one.

•

I wish I
could see the stars.

•

Trees *want*
to be still?
Winds
won't let them?

•

Anyhow,
it's night now.

Same clock ticks
in these different places.
                    3/1/76

ROBERT CREELEY

Old Magnolias

A mind made free in the Main Garden goes
slowly over the sense of what you've said.

Old magnolias burst into Latin –
white flowers flare, fall silent, leaves all

point to their divinity, a pink tree
thinks nothing of such perfection. The eye

leads naturally to where the sky is clearing
above the Sundial of Human Involvement

which can be located next
to the Observatory.

ANDREW   JOHNSTON

A Ballad of IHC

Two tourists were touring the Public Gardens.
     Under the native bush
They felt lovely cool and it smelt lovely sweet
And the everyday Wellington wind
       Was baffled, blanked, and thinned,
       As they strolled in the clamorous hush
       Under thousands of one-cricket bands.

They read the nametags and tried to learn
     One tree from another: Rewa-
Rewa was easy, its lance-tip leaves
     With ripply wicked edges;
And *Pittosporum* was a plant they knew
     From a hundred back-home hedges.

Although most of the names and shapes were strange
     To the aliens that they were,
Under the stamp-pad tree-ferns' fanned
     Umbrellas the great downpour
Of touring was shed and their spirits stirred,
Lifted by songs from this or that bird.

And when they came out at the top of the climb
     To the bottom of Glen Road,
They noticed a young Kiwi woman of one
     Of the pretty Kiwi sorts –
Fresh features, long blond windblown hair,

In everyday long black shorts.
She was canvassing door to door, with a bag
Lettered in black and white.
No business of theirs, they benignly thought,
They were only visitors, right?

On the third of a flight of steps she paused
Overtaking their smug idea,
Skipped down and over to them and said,
'I'm collecting for IHC.'
'What's IHC?' they asked, though now
(To be frank) they were pretty sure
They would give her something,
whatever it was,
But no harm in finding out, because
There are causes, and then there are causes.

'It's for Intellectually Handicapped
Children,' she said, at which
A light flipped on and a spirit rapped:
For reasons deeper than they would tell,
And buried beyond the Equator. Well,
They would give her something, no doubt of that,
The question now was, How much?

They studied their alien money – all
Faced by the youthful Queen
Who ruled from an island no longer Home
Around the planet twelve time zones.
Each bill was backed by a native bird
In yellow, blue, rose, or green –

Pigeon, Morepork, Tui they'd heard,
Takahe'd neither heard nor seen.

They pulled a green one out with a shrug,
      Hardly noticing what it was worth –
It was funny money, whatever the bird,
      On the nether side of the earth –
A 20, to give it its rightful number,
Which, by the current rate of exchange,
Was only eleven dollars US,
      Or even a little bit less.

Only? The girl turned crayfish pink:
      'Are you sure? I didn't mean
To hit you up –' So they had a quick think.
They still had plenty of birds in the bank,
And they thought it a simple way to thank
Aotearoa for taking them in,
Not to mention the one who once had been
In them, among them, and between,
      And they gave her the pigeon green.

JOHN RIDLAND

Wild Daisies

If you love me
Bring me flowers
Wild daisies
Clutched in your fist
Like a torch
No orchids or roses
Or carnations
No florist's bow
Just daisies
Steal them
Risk your life for them
Up the sharp hills
In the teeth of the wind
If you love me
Bring me daisies
Wild daisies
That I will cram
In a bright vase
And marvel at

BUB BRIDGER

The Windy Hills o' Wellington

The windy hills o' Wellington were black and cold that
     night,
The rain came down at times, enough to drown the
     'lectric light;
An' like a hymn of hate and want from black
     misfortune's choirs
I heard the cruel, spiteful wind go snarling thro' the
     wires.
An' from the winches by the wharf a rattle and a clank,
While sitting by a Sydney chum who's drawn
     New Zealand blank!

He'd sent for me, in all the land the only chum he knew,
His health and hope and cash were gone – and he was
     going too,
His frame was shrunk, his face was drawn, his eyes were
     blear'd and dim,
For drink and poverty and want had done their work for
     him;
And when I came, he turned to me, his features pale and
     lank –
'I'm glad you came, old chum,' he said, '*I've drawn
     New Zealand blank!*'

'"New leaf, new land", my motto was – I did my very
     best.
'Twas want of work that threw me back – an' liquor did
     the rest.

But nothing matters now, old man – it never did, no
      doubt
(Excuse a little nonsense when a fellow's peggin' out).
I'd live and fight if I had hope or money at the bank.
I've lived too long in '94, I've drawn New Zealand
      blank!'

I looked out through the window as the rain came
      pelting down;
The great black hills they seemed to close and loom
      above the town.
And in a strained and tired voice, that filled my heart
      with pain,
He said, 'Old man, I'd like to stroll down George Street
      once again.
I had myself to "battle" for; I've got myself to thank.
Perhaps it ain't New Zealand's fault that I've drawn
      New Zealand blank.'

The breezy hills o' Wellington are fair as they can be.
I stand and watch a Sydney boat go sailing out to sea.
And while the sun is setting low on blue and brown
      and green,
I think of cruel things that are, and things that might
      have been,
And while the same old sun goes down in clouds a
      golden bank,
I sadly think of my old chum who drew New Zealand
      blank.

No headstone marks his resting-place – no autumn
  grasses wave –
And not a sign of loving hands is seen above his grave;
For he recover'd from the spree – the doctors pulled
  him through;
His health came back and his luck turned (and so did
  my luck, too) –
He now has houses, land and shares, and thousands in
  the bank;
He doesn't know me now, because – I've drawn
  New Zealand blank.

'THE EXILE'
(HENRY LAWSON)

Unfamiliar Legends of the Stars

The wind turbine propels a sky
fighter grey above.

The tallest angel's head
curved the night.

A liquorice cable
wires hand to mouth.

Proud magpies
raced the dawn home.

Asphalt remains lively
weeks after its laying.

The water-girls laughed
and were exiled.

Things happen
and are wrapped in newspaper.

A seamstress sewed a spirit
from a bird's skin.

I put a ring around your name
and circle the globe.

KATE CAMP

Otari

A dark wind roars in the pines
The river runs over the stones
I am listening, lying alone
A morepork calls out to the stars.

The river runs over the stones
The rimu are creaking like masts
A morepork calls out to the stars
The frogs kak kak kak in the rushes.

The rimu are creaking like masts
The high tension wires are singing
The frogs kak kak kak in the rushes
The rain tat-tat-toos on the leaves.

The high tension wires are singing
The waterfalls burst and splatter
The rain tat-tat-toos on the leaves
The foxgloves are heavy and soft.

The waterfalls burst and splatter
A tui is sounding the morning
The foxgloves are heavy and soft
You used to lie here beside me.

A tui is sounding the morning
I am listening, lying alone
You used to lie here beside me
A dark wind roars in the pines.

LOUISE WRIGHTSON

The Acolyte

My quiet morning hill
   Stands like an altar drawn
Whereon hushed hands shall lay
   The shining pyx of dawn.

With penitence and stir,
   And drowsy flurry by,
The wind, a shamefaced serving-boy,
   Comes running up the sky.

EILEEN DUGGAN

Song in the Hutt Valley

Cirrus, stratus, cumulus,
Gentle or giant winds
Invoke the trees and cabbages;
The rising jet-trail finds
Space out of sight of valleys
Where the muddy rivers run
Past houses, groves and alleys
In the residential sun.

The placid eaves of evening
Purpled by homing sun
Pay little heed to reckoning
Broadcast by weathermen.
Houses still grow, the children
Like cabbages are seen;
Grandfather's thoughts are hidden
Upon the bowling green.

The sky's as much ambition
As anyone could eye,
Forecasts of nimbus, aeroplane
Pass over and pass by;
Tucked up at home, the passive
Who own their plot of ground
Sleep through the radio-active
Have a new formation found.

While history happens elsewhere
And few of us get hurt
Why should Grandad wish for hair
To line his sporting shirt?
His heart's at one with the children,
He can be overlooked
And left to play in the garden,
His place in heaven's booked.

The weather is established;
It will be wet – or fine –
The houses all are furnished –
In the styles of 'forty-nine.
No need to worry, hurry;
The questionmarks will keep;
The clouds and airmen marry
And the boisterous children sleep.

LOUIS JOHNSON

Waitangi Day, Porirua

The best place to be on Waitangi
Day is Porirua, and I gaze
up, and the clouds right above me have
elongated themselves, so they resemble
ribs, and I look out as if I am
inside the body. Taki, rua,
two moons in one small month and they are
calling them blue. Paua fritters three
dollars, big yellow blow-up bouncy
castle, flax bangles, sausage on a
stick, watermelon, eight guys in a
waka on the still lagoon. Bhuja.
An Indian woman sells me bhuja.
Porirua reggae is the best.
It is Bob Marley's birthday, *stir it*
up little darlin. The men wearing
lava lava beat the drums, the kids
jump in the fountain, *hangi be quick*
only four dollars for a good feed.

VIVIENNE PLUMB

Porirua Friday Night

Acne blossoms scarlet on their cheeks,
These kids up Porirua East. ...
Pinned across this young girl's breast
A name-tag on the supermarket badge;
A city-sky-blue smock.
Her face unclenches like a fist.

Fourteen when I met her first
A year ago, she's now left school,
Going with the boy
She hopes will marry her next year.
I asked if she found it hard
Working in the store these Friday nights
When friends are on the town.

    She never heard:
But went on, rather, talking of
The house her man had put
A first deposit on
And what it's like to be in love.

SAM HUNT

Titahi Bay

Not even ocean has this strange and vital glitter,
No mist, no rain, can keep these waves from glinting.
This is quick salt – this, alert water.

The Tasman enters here – it's wrath is white rage,
But when it comes between these cliffs it changes.
It is dire then: it is Maori.

Oh stealthy, silent, sure, like warriors descending,
Head up and tense, each wave pads swiftly inward.
This is swart brine – these are lithe breakers.

The gulls, their mats thrown back, are chary,
        deep and tribal.
They skirt the land like scouts upon a forage
And each breast gleams like an ice-crystal.

And when the battle breaks, what blows, what thuds,
        what clangour!
Against the cliffs' stockade, what roar of bodies!
And what sleep falls with the fray over!

And when these waters mourn, it is abandoned sorrow:
The billows tear themselves, upleaping, wailing,
In a stark woe, in a mad tangi.

This secret, flashing bay becomes in rip and current,
The dark but brilliant rune that is the Maori.
This is wild salt: this is wild water.

EILEEN DUGGAN

Threnody

In Plimmerton, in Plimmerton,
The little penguins play,
And one dead albatross was found
At Karehana Bay.

In Plimmerton, in Plimmerton,
The seabirds haunt the cave,
And often in the summertime
The penguins ride the wave.

In Plimmerton, in Plimmerton,
The penguins live, they say,
But one dead albatross they found
At Karehana Bay.

DENIS GLOVER

Memory Harbour

An image comes to me
of my grandmother.

Her dress is black.
So is her cardigan.

She sits in the living room
of my aunty's house in Titahi Bay.

I also see, a short distance
from the house,

three boatsheds.

Before the hill behind them
became a suburb

they were the only buildings
in the bay.

It was there
I caught herrings in milk bottles

beguiled
by the tide.

BRIAN GREGORY

Southerly

(for *Alexa*)

Waves crack like glass at Makara —
we watch behind perspex at the cafe.
Temuera swings from a fisherman's knot,
later he tackles the crawl and two-step.

Our tipuna walked here too. They passed over
unmarked stones, managed the shelled paua,
leap out in shapes. White noise is the breaker —
mumbling, and listening to it, our inheritance.

Kaikoura's chill breath and its Wellington
presence: principles, peninsulas, pamphlets,
the narrator steams to the capital. What blowing!
The Historic Story of Visitors (an abstract):

Deaths of whales, trees and people. Pigs
ashore. Gold petitions pans. Subdivision.
Guilt ends this (late, and too). Archives bear
the pall of those who knew 'the ancient ways'.

Few autographed their names. Settlers
wrote alpine tunes, Canterbury plainsongs,
bought bagpipes, noseflutes, and a Fomison.
Ah, South Island, your music remembers me.

ROBERT SULLIVAN

From Makara

This time it isn't cloud
whisked up, set into landscape
the kind that might trick
an inexperienced sailor

into sighting a fabulous coast.
Today the air is playing it
straight; and that is the white
of the South decorating the sky.

Some try to swim over;
or there's the quick route
along the cliff, winding up
through hebe and gorse

on a track that clutches so hard
it's worn to a groove
(the sea below laying out its net
of green and purple): to where

the batteries used to swing
from horizon to horizon.
Suddenly, the South sets out
to meet you, breaking

off into islands that strain
to become buoyant; opening up
its channels like the space
between arms to you:

Jump,

is the advice, launch yourself
into the gap; and something
will reach out far enough
to gather you across.

BILL SEWELL

Toroa: Albatross

Dedicated to those who found Albatross a home in Wellington

Day and night endlessly you have flown
Effortless of wing over chest expanding
Oceans far from land. Do you switch on
An automatic pilot, close your eyes
In sleep, Toroa?

On your way to your homeground at Otako heads
You tried to rest briefly on the Wai-te-mata
But were shot at by ignorant people. Crippled.
You find a resting place at Whanganui
A Tara; found space at last to recompose
Yourself

Now, without skin and flesh to hold you together
The division of your aerodynamic parts lie
Whitening, licked clean by sun and air and water.

Children will discover narrow corridors of
Airiness between, the suddenness of bulk;
Naked, laugh in the gush and ripple of your
Fountain.

You are not alone, Toroa. A taniwha once tried to break
Out of the harbour for the open sea. He failed
He is lonely
From the top of the mountain close
By he calls to you: *Welcome home, traveller*
Haere Mai
Your head tilts, your eyes open to the world.

H O N E   T U W H A R E

Biographical Notes

Fleur Adcock (1934–) lives in England where she works as a poet, editor and translator. She returns regularly to Wellington – where she was educated at Wellington Girls' College and Victoria University of Wellington.

James K. Baxter (1926–72) poet, playwright and social commentator, studied at Wellington Teachers' College and Victoria University of Wellington in the early 1950s. In September 1971, following the temporary cessation of his community at Jerusalem, Baxter returned to Wellington for several months.

Peter Bland poet and actor, was born in England in 1934. He moved to New Zealand in 1954 and studied English at Victoria University of Wellington (1955–59). Bland was co-founder of Downstage Theatre, Wellington, and its artistic director from 1964–68.

Jenny Bornholdt born in Lower Hutt in 1960, has published six books of poetry and co-edited two anthologies. Her most recent collection is *These Days* (Victoria University Press, 2000). She lives in Hataitai, Wellington.

Bub Bridger born in 1924 of Ngāti Kahungunu descent, began writing poetry late in life, following a visit to Ireland to trace family history. For many years she lived 'high in the sun' on a hill overlooking Wellington airport, and she now lives in Westport.

James Brown (1966–) is a Wellington-based poet and co-editor of the literary journal *Sport*. His second collection of poetry *Lemon* (Victoria University Press) was published in 1999. He was awarded a Buddle Findlay Sargeson Fellowship for 2000.

Rachel Bush lives in Nelson and completed the Original Composition course at Victoria University of Wellington in 1996. Her first collection was *The Hungry Woman* (Victoria University Press, 1997).

Kate Camp, born 1972, was educated at Victoria University of Wellington. Her debut collection *Unfamiliar Legends of the Stars* won the Jessie McKay Best First Book of Poetry, 1999 award. She lives in Newtown, Wellington.

Alistair Te Ariki Campbell, of Cook Island Maori descent, was born in Rarotonga in 1925 and has been writing poems for more than fifty years. His latest collection *Gallipoli & other poems* was published in 1999. For most of his life he has lived just north of Wellington at Pukerua Bay.

Geoff Cochrane published poetry in a number of small press collections, before his collection *Aztec Noon* appeared in 1992. Since then Victoria University Press has published his two novels and another collection, *Into India*. He was born in 1951 in Wellington where he still lives.

Robert Creeley (1926–) first visited New Zealand as a touring writer in 1976. He was a Fulbright Fellow at the University of Auckland in 1995, and has collaborated with New Zealand artist Max Gimblett on a book, *Dogs of Auckland*. Born in Massachusetts, he and his New Zealand-born wife live in Buffalo, New York.

Eileen Duggan (1894–1972) was, for a time, New Zealand's most internationally recognised poet. She was born in Tuamarina, Marlborough, then moved to Wellington for her tertiary education at Teachers' Training College and Victoria University College. She graduated in 1918 with a Masters degree in History, and remained in Wellington for the rest of her life.

Lauris Edmond (1924–2000) won the Commonwealth Poetry Prize in 1985 with her *Selected Poems*. Synonymous with Wellington and in particular Oriental Bay, Edmond was a vital presence in Wellington's literary life and wrote a celebrated three-volume autobiography.

David Eggleton (1952–) is a strong advocate of poetry as a performance. In 1985 he won London's *Time Out*'s Street Entertainer of the Year (Poetry) award. Eggleton is based in Dunedin, where much of his time is devoted to literary and art criticism.

Denis Glover (1912–1980) was an important literary figure from the 1930s onwards both as a poet and founder of the Caxton Press. He worked in Wellington at the *Dominion* (1937) and as an advertising copy-writer in 1954. His abiding love for the sea is reflected in the many poems he wrote about Wellington Harbour.

Brian Gregory spent his childhood in Wellington but has lived for some years in Auckland, where he writes and paints. Among his many small press publications are *Katherine Mansfield*, *Our Missing Contemporary* (Puriri Press, 1991) and *In Winter Vineyards* (Pear Tree Press, 1999), which was illustrated by Richard McWhannell.

Dinah Hawken (1943–) lives in the Wellington suburb of Northland. Her first collection *It Has No Sound and Is Blue* won the 1987 Commonwealth (Poetry) Prize for Best First Book. Her other books include *Small Stories of Devotion* (1991) and *Water, Leaves, Stones* (1995).

Sam Hunt was born in Auckland in 1946. He lived for many years on the Pauatahanui Inlet, just north of Wellington, where he was part of a group of artists, poets and writers known as the 'Bottle Creek' community. He now lives 'up North', still close to the sea.

Robin Hyde was the pen name for Iris Wilkinson (1906–1939). 'The Beaches' is part of a longer poem, 'Houses by the Sea', begun in New Zealand, completed in England and published many years after her untimely death. Her short but prolific writing career in poetry, fiction and journalism began in Wellington, where she worked as a parliamentary reporter for the *Dominion* 1925–26.

Louis Johnson (1924–1988) was a journalist, editor, teacher and poet. As a young man Johnson was part of the 'Wellington Group' of poets which included Baxter and Campbell. In 1951 he founded the *New Zealand Poetry Yearbook*. In 1980 he became the second writing fellow at Victoria University of Wellington, and several years later held the Katherine Mansfield Memorial Fellowship at Menton.

Andrew Johnston, born in 1963, grew up in the Hutt Valley. He edited the books page of Wellington's *Evening Post* for several years and published his first book of poetry, *How to Talk*, in 1993. He now lives in Paris, where he works on the *Herald Tribune*.

August Kleinzahler (1949–) is an award-winning American poet, who first visited New Zealand in 1992 at which time he wrote 'Sunday, Across the Tasman'. He returned as a guest to Writers and Readers Week at the International Festival of the Arts in 1998. The poem was first published in *Sport*.

Fiona Kidman (1940–) is one of New Zealand's most celebrated novelists. She has also published short stories, plays and poetry. 'Speaking with my Grandmothers' was first published in *Writing Wellington* (Victoria University Press, 1999).

Henry Lawson (1867–1922) was an Australian short-story writer, journalist and poet. He is believed to have written 'The Windy Hills o'Wellington', which was published in the *New Zealand Times* on 27 January 1894, and attributed to 'The Exile'. Lawson visited Wellington during the 1893 depression, and again several years later with his wife. Their son was born in Wellington.

Rachel McAlpine was born in Fairlie in 1940. A prolific poet, novelist and playwright, she now lives in Wellington. Recent non-fiction includes *Web Word Wizardry*.

Bill Manhire (1946–) is Professor of English at Victoria University of Wellington, and instigator of the internationally renowned Creative Writing programme. Manhire is one of this country's leading poets and his latest collection is *What to call your child* (Godwit, 1999).

Katherine Mansfield, pen-name of Kathleen Beauchamp, was born in Wellington in 1888 and died in France in 1923. She was educated at Wellington Girls' College and Miss Swainson's private school, and in London at Queen's College. She returned to Wellington in 1906 before her final departure for Europe in 1908. The 'library' in the first line of 'Vignette – Through the Autumn afternoon' is thought to be the Parliamentary Library in Wellington, where she often read.

Ronald L. Meek 'An M.P.'s Life for Me' was published in the banned 1940 Victoria University College Extravaganza 'Jonnalio'.

Stephanie de Montalk (1945–) launched her first poetry collection, *Animals Indoors* (Victoria University Press) in 2000. She is currently working on a biography of her cousin, Count Geoffrey Potocki de Montalk, poet and pretender to the Polish throne.

Michael Morrissey was born in Auckland in 1942. He has published widely as a poet, fiction writer, reviewer and essayist. He edited *The Flamingo Anthology of New Zealand Short Stories*, published in 2000.

W. H. Oliver (1925–) is a widely published historian, Professor of History at Massey University (1964–83) and General Editor of the first volume of the *Dictionary of New Zealand Biography*. He has also published three books of poetry.

Bob Orr (1949–) has, since the early 1970s, published his work in many journals and anthologies. His most recent collection is *Breeze* (Auckland University Press, 1992). Most of his working life has been on the Auckland waterfront.

Chris Orsman was born in Lower Hutt in 1955. He studied and worked as an architect but now works as a parliamentary chauffeur. A revised version of his second book of poetry, *South* (1966), was published by Faber and Faber in London (1999). In 1996 Orsman co-founded Pemmican Press, producing small editions by established and emerging poets.

Vincent O'Sullivan (1937–) has published poetry, short fiction, novels, and plays, for which he has received many awards and prizes. He is Director of the Stout Research Centre at Victoria University of Wellington.

Vivienne Plumb was born in Sydney, Australia in 1955. Wellington-based, she writes prose, drama and poetry, and has won awards in all three fields.

Lindsay Rabbit opens his collection *upagainstit* (Voice Press, 1983), with 'letter from holloway road'. He has also published *On the Line* in 1985 and *thewayofit* in 1988. He works as a freelance writer on the Kapiti Coast.

John Ridland (1933–) is a Californian poet who published his first book of poetry in 1961. His wife, Muriel Thomas, is a New Zealander. 'A Ballad for IHC' was written during a visit to Wellington in 1992. Ridland teaches writing and literature at the University of California, in Santa Barbara.

Iain Sharp (1953–) published three collections of poems in the 1980s. He has lived in Auckland much of his life, although he spent a formative year at Library School in Wellington.

C. K. Stead (1932–) formerly Professor of English at Auckland University, has written novels, criticism and poetry. In the 1950s he aligned himself with Allen Curnow in opposition to the 'Wellington Group' of poets. Stead's *Straw Into Gold: Poems New and Selected* appeared in 1997, and a new collection *The Right Thing* early in 2000.

Bill Sewell was born in Athens in 1951. He studied German at Auckland University and obtained a law degree at Victoria University of Wellington. He now works as a freelance writer, editor and reviewer in Wellington and co-edits *New Zealand Books*.

J. C. Sturm (1927–) is a short story writer and poet. She published her first poem in 1947, one of the first Maori (Taranaki iwi) women to appear in print. Her most recent collection is *Postscripts* (Steele Roberts, 2000). Sturm lives at Paekakariki, north of Wellington.

Robert Sullivan born 1967, of Nga Puhi and Irish descent, published his first book of poems in 1990, *Jazz Waiata*. This was followed in 1993 with *Piki Ake* and *Star Waka* in 1999.

Hone Tuwhare (1922–) began his career as a poet while working as a boilermaker on Waikato River hydroelectric projects in the mid 1950s. Born in Kaikohe, Tuwhare now lives at Kaka Point, South Otago. Tuwhare wrote 'Toroa: Albatross' to mark the official presentation of Tanya Ashken's sculpture on the Wellington waterfront in May 1986.

Ian Wedde (1946–) moved to Wellington in 1975, having travelled widely in New Zealand and overseas. He has published extensively in poetry, fiction, art and literary criticism, in addition to co-editing two anthologies of New Zealand verse. In 1994 he became arts projects manager at the Museum of New Zealand Te Papa Tongarewa.

Damien Wilkins was born in Lower Hutt in 1963, and educated at Victoria University of Wellington and Washington University, Missouri, where he completed an MFA in Creative Writing. Wilkins has published short stories, novels and a collection of poems *The Idles* (Victoria University Press, 1993). He lives in Newtown, Wellington.

David McKee Wright (1869–1928) was born in the north of Ireland and came to New Zealand in 1887. After farming in Otago, he trained for the Congregational Ministry and served as a pastor in Wellington before breaking with the Church in 1905. Wright then worked as a freelance journalist in Nelson before moving to Australia. His ballads are widely anthologised and valued within their historical context.

Louise Wrightson (1948–) lives in Wellington, near Otari, Wilton Bush. Her poem is a pantoum, written while she was a student of Bill Manhire's Creative Writing course at Victoria University of Wellington.